HOPE

GATHERED

GOD'S PROMISES FOR FAMILIES

WITH CHILDREN WHO ARE

SICK, DISABLED, OR HOSPITALIZED

D1512169

TOMMY SCHROCK

FOREWORD BY COACH GENE STALLINGS

EDITED BY DR. LANGSTON HAYGOOD

Hope Gathered

God's Promises for Families with Children who are Sick, Disabled, or Hospitalized

Tommy Schrock

Foreword by Coach Gene Stallings

Edited by Dr. Langston Haygood

ISBN: 9781795521000

Edited by Dr. Langston Haygood. Additional editing by Diane Simmons Dill and Angela Skelton.

Cover and interior artwork by Sarah Nunnally. Used by permission.

Interior design and formatting by Diane Simmons Dill and Angela Skelton.

PRINTED IN THE UNITED STATES OF AMERICA

WHAT OTHERS ARE SAYING

"Through my career in pediatric healthcare I have seen the stress and despair borne by parents and families of children who face serious medical conditions. *Hope Gathered* is the product of one family's experience and provides a framework for coping with the challenges through prayer and a better understanding of God's love. I believe it can be an important resource and comfort to those in need."

Tom Shufflebarger, Chief Operating Officer, Children's Hospital, Birmingham, Alabama

"In his book, Tommy Schrock encourages the reader by providing Biblical truths to equip you with answers to some of life's most difficult questions. He helps us see where hope comes from...Hope comes from God. I recommend to anyone who has just received difficult news to spend time daily reading through this book."

Chris Hunsberger, Executive Director, Radical, *https://radical.net/*

"I can think of no one more eminently qualified to speak to and encourage others on how to shepherd, love and parent a child with special needs than Tommy and Terri Schrock.

The Lord entrusted Caitlin to them for almost 18 years, where they modeled Christ to her and to the world! These biblically based devotions are life changing and of such a blessing and are a wonderful study. Thank you, Tommy and Terri, for your insights into God's Word and for your transparency."

Tim Prewitt, Senior Director, World Reach,
http://world-reach.org/

"*Hope Gathered* is a powerful testimony of faith—the confidence in what we hope for, and assurance about what we do not see (Hebrews 11:1)—that penetrates the heart and provides encouragement, promise, and peace through uncertain times and difficult situations. Through these powerful and meaningful devotions built on personal experiences, Tommy carries hope through the light of Jesus and provides affirmation that God is always at work.

Ultimately, these devotions are a testament that Caitlin is still impacting lives both near and far, and that her legacy of drawing people towards Jesus continues on in mighty ways."

Josh Duncan, USA Director, MountainChild,
https://mountainchild.org/

"Anyone with families of special needs children or loved ones sick and in the hospital will treasure *Hope Gathered*. This heart-written, moving testimony is filled with God's Word of promises that provide answers to hard questions and comfort during difficult times."

Suzanne Owens, Executive Director, Sozo Children, *http://www.sozochildren.org/*

"In my life, whenever I have faced difficult times, it is the constant assurance of knowing that God is with me that gets me through. *Hope Gathered* will remind you that God's promises never fail because God never fails. These promises from God's Word were gathered by one who has been in your shoes and gone through the most painful times imaginable of losing a child. Yet, Tommy Schrock's testimony is that God never failed his precious Caitlin and God never let him and his family down. Indeed, God is good and through these short inspirational devotions I believe God will remind you of His unbelievable goodness as well."

Randy Norris, Pastor, The Station Church, Birmingham, Alabama

"*Hope Gathered* is the ideal gift for those who find themselves in a season of overwhelming need. I recommend it wholeheartedly."

David Nasser, Pastor and Author, *A Call to Die*

"God puts certain special people in our lives at certain times. Nothing He does is by mistake or coincidence. Tommy and Terri Schrock are two of those special people for many, but certainly to our family in our journey. *Hope Gathered* is a product of God's work in Tommy, and this product resulted in a devotional for families with children who are sick, disabled, or hospitalized. A rough draft stayed at our son's bedside table in his hospital room, and helped anchor my family through stormy seas."

Walker Moss, Family Friend and Father

"Tommy Schrock and his wife, Terri, know all about discouragement and sorrow. Their daughter, Caitlin, was born with Trisomy 18, an uncommon chromosome disorder. Through this book, *Hope Gathered*, Tommy reaches out to families with sick, disabled, and/or hospitalized children with Scriptural encouragement and personal stories of hope. It is a beautifully-written book of daily devotions penned by a Christian father who found God's amazing love and hope when he and his family most needed it. I highly recommend *Hope Gathered* for a family's personal devotion material as well as a gift to give hope and encouragement to other families."

Denise George, Author, *Teach Your Children to Pray*

TABLE OF CONTENTS

DEDICATION

To "Baby Cakes" Caitlin,

I could fill books thanking you for all the things God has taught me through you. Thank you for bringing me out of the false security of self so I could find the hope only found in Jesus. I miss and love you like crazy.

To Terri, my amazing wife,

Our family was blessed with Caitlin because of your heart. The girls and I have seen Christ-like love through you. Thank you for showing us what selfless, unconditional love looks like every day. For 17 years we saw you put Caitlin's needs in front of your own. You have loved Caitlin well. I am so thankful for you. I love you.

To my girls, with love: Courtney, Megan, and Macey,

I cherish having seen Caitlin be your "normal." You have tube-fed, hugged seizures, and pushed a wheelchair countless times. While the world watched, you wondered why they were staring. Caitlin was blessed to have you as sisters. I am grateful to God for the positive impact she has had in your life. It is with the deepest love and most profound pride that I'm blessed to be your daddy.

FOREWORD

On June 11, 1962, my wife, Ruth Ann, and I were blessed and delighted as our baby boy Johnny was born. I brought Ruth Ann some flowers to the hospital room, but she seemed distracted. She said, "Bebes, everyone else in the ward has seen their baby, but they haven't brought ours yet. Would you go out and ask the doctor if anything is wrong?" I went to find the doctor, and he quickly told me, "Yes, we think maybe your baby is a mongoloid (years later 'Down syndrome' replaced 'mongoloid')." The information was stunning and frustrating with its delivery. I passed out from the shock. When I awoke, I had to deliver the news to my wife. At first, I couldn't even speak. Finally, the words came, "Ruthie, the doctor just gave us some bad news." Ruth Ann began to cry.

What started as a day of celebration turned into a day of medical terms fogging the mind and putting a painful knot in the pit of my stomach. Everything seemed suspended in slow motion as waves of thoughts and emotions came. I prayed to God to change Johnny, but God changed me.

We had begun a journey that was not planned by us but purposed by God; a life where Johnny would influence and impact not only our lives but the lives of all those around him. My life would not have been nearly as rich if I had not had Johnny. If the good Lord would let me go back and have a perfectly healthy boy or take Johnny, I would take Johnny every time.

I am grateful for Tommy Schrock writing a devotional book specifically for families with children who have special needs, are sick, or in the hospital. From the life experiences with his daughter, Caitlin, he

3

understands how to come alongside these families with encouragement. When news and circumstances regarding a child overcome families, there isn't the time or attention to do anything else but get through the day. Tommy has written *Hope Gathered* devotionals specifically for these difficult times. Each devotional presents a specific promise from God for their situation. These promises bring hope that will encourage and strengthen families as they move forward into a new story God has given them.

Coach Gene Stallings, Author of *Another Season*

HOPE

gathered

PREFACE

*So they gathered them up and filled
twelve baskets with fragments from the
five barley loaves left by those who had
eaten.*

JOHN 6:13

As Jesus commanded the disciples to gather the leftover bread, so He has put on my heart to gather His promises for families with a child who is sick, disabled, or hospitalized. I pray that these precious promises of God, found only in Christ Jesus, prove to be the hope and peace that comfort your spirit.

These devotionals were intentionally kept short. May these small portraits of God's love and grace be a comfort when times make it hard to focus or pray. Think of them as a spiritual "mint" to savor throughout the day.

WHY GATHER PROMISES?

I have been in the hospital with my children, knowing that God loves me, and I have found very specific promises that He led me to in His Word. Through experience, these specific promises have proved to be a firm anchor that held me steady, despite the storm.

During my last hospital visit, the Lord put on my heart to collect these promises for your family. I have done all I can to get myself out of the way so that you might see more clearly the Hope found in His Word. I have most likely been praying for you before you even knew this season would come into your life. My heart hurts for you and your family. Having walked this path before you, this is my way of giving you a "spiritual hug" from my heart to yours to encourage you on the journey you are on now.

The quote below by Thomas Brooks sums up well what I've tried to do in this book.[1] As you gather God's precious promises, may your heart and soul drink deeply from the comfort and satisfaction found only in God's Word.

> These spiritual and absolute promises are of nearest and greatest concernment to you; ... these are of greatest use to satisfy you, and to settle you when you are wavering; to support you when you are falling; to recall you when you are wandering; to comfort you when you are fainting; and to counsel you when you are staggering. Therefore make these your choicest and your chiefest companions ... sit down at this fire, and be warmed; drink of these springs, and be satisfied; taste of the delicacies, and be cheered.[2]
>
> Thomas Brooks, *Heaven on Earth*

---

[1] Note: The spacing for this quote has been altered for easier reading.

[2] Thomas Brooks, *Heaven on Earth*, 6th ed. (East Peoria IL: Versa Press, 2015), 199.

Hope Gathered Through Caitlin

He will tend his flock like a shepherd; he will gather the lambs in his arms; he will carry them in his bosom [close to His heart], and gently lead those that are with young.

ISAIAH 40:11

JESUS WILL CARRY YOU

Our daughter Caitlin was two days old when our world turned upside down. We were still at the hospital, and the doctor presented a scan of Caitlin's heart. The scan loomed into view as we stood, staring at the undeniable truth: Caitlin's heart had two sizable holes. Then the bigger truth: the holes had to be corrected, or Caitlin would die. I was crushed by the enormity of the situation. A parent's worst nightmare. My child had a severe health complication.

My heart and soul broken, the faulty foundation of self-reliance and self-dependence shattered into pieces. Trying to make sense out of something that made no sense, my brain felt numb

The doctor said, "Do you want me to tell Terri," my wife, "or do you want to?" I got up to carry the worst news my wife could hear. I remember the weight of heartbreak, sadness, and panic as I walked into our room.

There are times when it seems impossible to carry on. The promise is in those moments—Jesus will carry us. Jesus loves us and will minister to all our needs. When we are crushed, He wraps His arms around us, comforting us and cushioning us from life's harshest blows. We are embraced. Jesus hugs us close to His heart. He brings us through. The One whose arms carried a cross will carry you through the hour of deepest need.

PRAY

Lord Jesus, when I feel like I cannot go on, You can. You have loved me through your suffering, even to your grave. You have risen in power. I trust you for strength and comfort in this hour of desperation. Carry me so that I will go on. Hug me close that I may keep hope in You. I rest in Your arms. I know You are here. I pray in the Name of Jesus, Amen.

Read Further: Isaiah 41:13; 46:4; 63:9; Galatians 2:20; Romans 8:32

FOR THE FAMILY

Share the Scripture and reflect on the promise with your family. Discuss a memorable hug that made you feel better. How satisfying is it to know that Jesus hugs our hearts during hard times? Christ promises He wraps His arms around us. He will pull us close to His heart, and He will not let go. He promises to carry us through whatever difficulties we have.

How has Jesus shown us that He loves us?

NOTES, REFLECTIONS, PRAYERS

HOPE
gathered

He gives power to the faint, and to him
who has no might he increases strength.

ISAIAH 40:29

STRENGTH

Our baby Caitlin was four days old. We had just arrived at a neonatal care hospital, still reeling from the diagnosis and the impact it was already having on our whole family.

The doctors rushed into the room and began examining her. They told us, "Caitlin has a cyst on her kidney that needs surgery, and she has a twist in her bowel. We do not think she can see or hear. Her heart is not oriented properly. Caitlin will need heart surgery."

We were directed to the waiting room so the doctors could do more examinations. We had not been home since Caitlin was born. My wife, Terri, and I were already exhausted. This new information was more than we could bear. Crushed, we could not express our emotions. All we could do was stand in the middle of the room and cling to each other. People walked around us. We felt dazed and separated from the world.

How is a parent to go on in such a situation? We felt it was more than we could endure. Crisis calls for mental and physical strength. In Isaiah 40:29, we are promised God will hold us up by His comfort and wisdom. He is truly our comfort, strength, and understanding. Such devastating news buckles our knees. Fainting, we look for help, and God's arms embrace us. When we are puzzled and desperate, His understanding is our guide.

He carries us. We may faint and fall into the arms of God. He is there. He promises to give us the strength we need.

PRAY

Father, You are the God that gives strength to the weak. You carry me when I cannot go on. When my strength has failed, You will hold me. Lord, I rest in Your might. May my soul be strengthened in the hope that I have in You. In the precious Name of Jesus, Amen.

Read Further: Isaiah 40:11, 28

FOR THE FAMILY

Share the Scripture and reflect on the promise with your family. Discuss a time you lost electrical power to your house during a storm. Talk about how the electrical company looked for where the source of power had been broken in order to restore electricity to your home. We are promised God will restore our strength when we feel powerless.

How does God comfort us in the midst of our pain?

NOTES, REFLECTIONS, PRAYERS

HOPE
gathered

You have decided the length of our lives.
You know how many months we will live,
and we are not given a minute longer.

JOB 14:5 NLT

OUR LIFE'S PURPOSE WILL BE FULFILLED

Caitlin was eight days old. We were still at the neonatal care hospital and the doctors had to figure out her underlying health problem. When the news finally came, the nurse walked us to a room. Several specialists and doctors sat quietly around a conference table. The attending doctor said, "The news is not good. Caitlin has Trisomy 18. She will only live about six to eight more weeks. You can carry her home on hospice and make the necessary preparations for her burial." Stunned. Desperate. We began asking questions trying to find some trace of hope. The doctors were very compassionate, but there was no hope in the blunt words hanging in our hearts like heavy weights.

Surprise! Caitlin lived almost eighteen years. The Lord used her to make the most significant impact in each of her family member's lives.

In Job 14:5, we see that only God knows the length of our days. Our final and full story is unknown and will not end until its appointed time with the appropriate fulfillment. God is continually involved in each of our lives, designed before we were born. He has a unique plan for us. Our purpose will be completed in accordance with His plan.

PRAY

Father, You are my God and the Author
of my life. Bring to me the peace that
comes from knowing You have a plan for
my child. I might not see or understand
what is going on, but my trust and hope
are in You. May You be glorified in the
days you have given to me and my child.
I pray in Jesus' Name, Amen.

Read Further: Psalm 139:16; Galatians 1:15;
Jeremiah 1:5

FOR THE FAMILY

Share the Scripture and reflect on the promise with your family. Discuss your family's favorite book and talk about how it ends. What if the author stopped writing halfway through the book? How would that impact the whole story?

Who is the author of our story? When was our story written? We have a purpose and will fulfill it according to His design within the days He has given us.

In what ways is God already using your story to touch others?

NOTES, REFLECTIONS, PRAYERS

As he passed by, he saw a man blind from birth. And his disciples asked him, "Rabbi, who sinned, this man or his parents, that he was born blind?" Jesus answered, "It was not that this man sinned, or his parents, but that the works of God might be displayed in him."

JOHN 9:1-3

A SPECIAL PLAN

Caitlin was born with Trisomy 18, an uncommon chromosome disorder which led to profound special needs. She lived with us for seventeen years before parting to the presence of the Lord. Though she could never walk or talk, God displayed Himself daily in her life. Her story is one that kept the doctors astonished. The last doctor to see her said, "I know enough about Caitlin not to try and tell you what is going to happen and when."

Our family would have never chosen to have a child with special needs. But Caitlin showed us God knew exactly what we needed. He allows us to go through hard times. Times we would not choose or understand, but He sees the whole picture and uses them to shape us into who He wants. For example, Caitlin has three sisters: Macey, Courtney, and Megan. As I write this, Macey is on a mission trip. She is sharing how God used Caitlin to point her toward the hope of heaven. Tuesday, Courtney accepted her first job. She will be a special needs teacher. Megan wants to work with children who are sick.

God used Caitlin in my heart to push pride aside so I would seek Him. Caitlin taught her mom that although it can sometimes seem that God gives us more than we can handle, He won't leave us there. He does not abandon us to care for our children alone. He inspires us to lean on Him, trust and be amazed at what He can do.

In John 9:1-3, God does not hide those that are sick or disabled, but through them displays His sovereign and merciful hand to the world. Sickness and disability are not the end of hope but begin a special hope: a special promise. God uses sickness and disability to show Himself. We did not know God's plan for Caitlin, but we had the privilege of having a front row seat to watch God unveil His special love and power. God entrusted us with Caitlin, and through her, impacted our lives and the lives of others forever.

PRAY

Father, I pray that You would show Your mighty hand in the life of (_____). I do not understand everything, but I trust in Your promises and know that I will be amazed at what You do. Use me to make Your name known and draw all to You. Fill me with Your love that all will know you are the only true God and living hope. Give me the strength and wisdom needed to navigate the special plan You have for me. In Jesus' Name I pray, Amen.

Read further: Psalm 139:13-16; Exodus 4:11; John 9

FOR THE FAMILY

Share the Scripture and reflect on the promise in John 9:1-3 with your family. Talk about the time someone you loved was in need. How did you meet that need?

God loves us. Our love for others becomes visible when we help them in their time of distress. One way in which God shows His love is by helping us when we need it most. God might not help in the way we want or expect, but the promise is that He comes into our sickness and disability.

In what ways does God use sickness and disability to make Himself known to influence your life and the lives of others?

NOTES, REFLECTIONS, PRAYERS

_____

_____

_____

_____

_____

_____

HOPE
gathered

If you need wisdom, ask our generous
God, and he will give it to you.

JAMES 1:5 NLT

A WISE DECISION

Caitlin was three weeks old. We carried her home from the hospital with a feeding tube, oxygen tank and heart monitor. Constrained by cords and tubes, we couldn't move her beyond their reach. The doctors said she had a few weeks to live. Her breathing was declining daily. Terri wanted to remove the monitoring and oxygen equipment: her passion was to hold and hug Caitlin freely, take her outside, and let Caitlin's sister hold her without all the tubes in the way. We discussed if we should. But doing this could hasten Caitlin's death.

I went outside to pray. Peace flowed. I knew removing the equipment is what we should do. We removed it all. We had a perfect family day, a day outdoors, loving our daughter. The next day Caitlin's breathing improved. We later learned the oxygen was causing the problem because of a heart complication.

How does a parent make the right decision? James 1:5 clearly illustrates one of God's promises to help. He is the source and supplier of wisdom. When our minds are troubled, God does not abandon us. He knows how critical each choice can be because He made the most difficult decision a Father could make when He sent His only Son to die on the cross for us. God promises to give us understanding of what to do. When we trust Him to help make a decision, He is there. God generously provides the guidance we need.

PRAY

Father, Your wisdom knows no end. I surrender my decisions to You. Make clear the way I should go. Give me insight into this situation. Give me peace for the path. In the precious Name of Jesus, I pray, Amen.

Read Further: James 1:6; Proverbs 2:6-8; Colossians 2:2-3

FOR THE FAMILY

Share the Scripture and reflect on the promise with your family. Discuss how much training and education your doctor has had. Use this time to thank God for your physician. Your doctor is committed to helping you make the right medical decisions. In James 1:5, we learn God is also committed to helping us through difficult choices. The God who knows all, promises to guide you along the path.

Who has trained or educated God? Discuss the meaning of wisdom and how He leads us to it.

NOTES, REFLECTIONS, PRAYERS

HOPE
gathered

[H]e will give you everything you need.
"So don't worry about tomorrow, for
tomorrow will bring its own worries.
Today's trouble is enough for today."

MATTHEW 6:33-34 NLT

PROVISION

Terri asked me, "Tommy, what are we going to do if Caitlin needs a colostomy bag?" Questions and worries swirled through our heads. This development would affect not only Caitlin, but our entire family. Having never dealt with such an issue, we had no idea what to expect.

Terri and I worried a lot about the "what ifs" and other prospective problems. As Caitlin grew, how would we be able to carry her? What happens when she gets too big for grocery cart seats? How are we going to do family vacations? Is Caitlin going to be sick all the time? How is she going to affect her sisters? Can we handle all the staring from others? We both were worriers and made it a full-time occupation early on with Caitlin.

In reality, our "what ifs" weren't the issue: We didn't see the complications coming. Caitlin started having seizures. She threw up again and again, even though she could not eat by mouth. She developed scoliosis. She had portal hypertension. As the complications mounted, God taught us through Caitlin there will always be problems. We had to learn to trust Him daily and not worry about what wasn't there.

In Matthew 6:33-34, Jesus teaches us that our worries will begin to wither. Jesus says our heavenly Father knows our needs. Two things come on a daily basis: One is trouble; the other is provision from our Father. He gives in proportion to today's problem.

Tomorrow has not come. God will provide what we need today. Our part is to continually trust in Him.

PRAY

Father, I praise You for being a loving Father. You know my every need. You give me exactly what is required to get through the day. May my hope and trust be found in You alone. May I rest in this truth. I ask You to wash away the worries that fill my mind, and help me to fully trust in You. I pray in Jesus' Name, Amen.

Read Further: Lamentations 3:21-23

FOR THE FAMILY

Share the Scripture and reflect on the promise with your family. Talk about how your family would travel on a plane. The children would not be given their ticket prior to the flight. They don't need it. It might be lost. The ticket is given when necessary. They receive it as they board the plane. So our Father in heaven gives us what we need at the proper time. We can trust He will give us what we need when we need it and we do not have to worry about tomorrow.

How can we not worry by trusting God? What does it mean to not worry? What does it mean to trust God?

NOTES, REFLECTIONS, PRAYERS

_____

_____

_____

_____

_____

_____

_____

_____

_____

_____

_____

_____

HOPE
gathered

*Your testimonies are my delight; they
are my counselors.*

PSALM 119:24

GOOD COUNSEL

After a doctor's visit for Caitlin, Terri said, "You won't believe the suggestion the nurse gave me today." The look on her face told me it was a ridiculous thought to her.

"What did the nurse suggest?" I asked.

She said, "You and Tommy should not have any more children."

A bit stunned by this suggestion from a professional in the medical field, I asked Terri what she thought about that. She replied, "I don't feel that is God's plan for us."

After Terri and I had Caitlin, we began to get a lot of advice. People who were not even close to us would let us know how we should live our lives. The nurse was giving us what she thought was the right counsel. She probably didn't think we could handle a child with special needs, Caitlin's sister, and another baby. Thankfully, our ears were tuned to God. We went on to have two more children and could not imagine our world without them.

In Psalm 119:24, we see that the Psalmist's delight is in the guidance found in God's voice through His Word. People mean well when giving advice, and the opinions of others have value. However, the course of action and the direction of any decision should be grounded in the wise advice found in Scripture. We regard what others say, but we also recognize the path to any conclusion is through prayer and meditation in God's Word.

PRAY

Father, I thank You for Your Word and the direction it gives me. When there are so many voices in my head telling me what to do, help me to see the way in which You would lead me. Fill me with the delight and confidence in knowing You are, indeed, my special Counselor. Guide my decisions so that I may glorify You and rejoice in Your glory. In the matchless Name of Jesus, Amen.

Read further: Psalm 73:24; 33:11, Isaiah 40:13

FOR THE FAMILY

Share the Scripture and reflect on the promise with your family. Every device that can play music comes with a volume control. When a song we like comes on that device, we turn up the volume. It's like the advice we listen to when considering what to do. We may very well listen to friends and family. God blesses us through the people around us to give good counsel. However, before any conclusion, we should tune into the Word of God and listen to the volume of His voice.

How may we seek the counsel of God for any decision? How can we hear Him?

NOTES, REFLECTIONS, PRAYERS

_____

_____

_____

_____

_____

_____

_____

_____

_____

_____

_____

HOPE
gathered

Moses' arms soon became so tired he could no longer hold them up. So Aaron and Hur found a stone for him to sit on. Then they stood on each side of Moses, holding up his hands. So his hands held steady until sunset.

Exodus 17:12 NLT

A HELPING HAND

Our family received the responsibility of caring for our daughter Caitlin. There was no way we could have tended to her alone. Throughout Caitlin's life, God brought the most amazing people into our journey who helped us.

These people came alongside, supporting and encouraging us. For example, nurses who always knew what to say after doctors delivered devastating reports, and doctors who followed up our visits with phone calls of love and concern. Then there were family members who shouldered the challenge; teachers who poured their lives into caring for Caitlin each day. They loved her. Friends embraced us as family. Churches covered us with prayer, care and love. God seemed to give us more than we could handle but He hugged us and held up our hands through others. A "bear hug" from the body of Christ.

In Exodus 17:12, Moses received a task that was more than he could manage. For the people of Israel to have success, he was required to hold his staff high. The struggle was lengthy but his strength was brief. The promise is God gives us the help we need for our new challenge. He gave Moses two companions. They journeyed with him up a difficult mountain. They stood by him! They held his arms up as his strength drained down. They shared the burden. The result was daily strength.

PRAY

Father, I thank You for those You put in my life. Those whom You have given the heart to come alongside and love my family well. I am blessed to have so many who care. Enable me to be transparent and to share the burdens of my heart and life. Give me humility and wisdom to allow others to help me. Hold and hug me close through these people who faithfully journey with me. In the Name of Jesus, Amen.

Read Further: Exodus 17:8-13

FOR THE FAMILY

Share the Scripture and promise with your family: A Promise of a Helping Hand. Talk about the people who care for you when you are in the hospital. When we are weak, we need help. God has given each of these people a heart to do what they do. He provides them with the skill to meet your needs. God has sent them to care for you.

Will God give you the people in your life to love and help you to meet your challenge? Whom has God provided already to help you meet that challenge? By the way: Have you thanked that person?

NOTES, REFLECTIONS, PRAYERS

_____

_____

_____

_____

_____

_____

_____

_____

_____

_____

_____

_____

HOPE
gathered

*[L]et us run with endurance the race
that is set before us, looking to Jesus, the
founder and perfecter of our faith.*

HEBREWS 12:1-2

ENDURANCE

The other day I asked Terri, "How were you able to care for Caitlin so well over all these years?"

She answered, "Jesus."

Simple, yet profound, her answer did not surprise me. As Caitlin's mom, Terri ran her race with endurance. Tending to a daughter who has special needs is not easy. Caitlin could not walk or talk. For seventeen years our family watched Terri freely put Caitlin's needs before her own. Terri loved her. If both were hungry, Terri fed Caitlin first. She dressed her first; Caitlin looked pristine. Time and attention given to her hair! Wow.

If Terri herself received cash as a gift, she would use it to buy something special for Caitlin. Terri loved, prayed over, carried and cared for, held close, and poured herself out for her daughter. Where does a mother find this endless endurance for such a race?

Love. Love was her motive. Jesus was her strength. In Hebrews 12:1-2, we see the promise that Jesus endured the race, and following his example, it enables us to endure it as well. How does He enable us? He develops our love for Him. We trust Him as we run. He gives the endurance. Terri learned to surrender all to the Lord. She loved who loved her. She ran her race holding His hand, resting in His help, relying on His strength.

PRAY

Jesus, I look to You for the strength and stamina for the race You have set before me. I trust, but I ask You to inspire my trust even more. Give me the patience and endurance to love (_____) as Christ loved us, and the fortitude to meet the needs that are before me. May I look to You so my hope will be raised, my confidence affirmed, and my faith perfected. In the Name of Jesus, I pray, Amen.

Read Further: Hebrews 11; 12:1-2; Matthew 7:12; 25:35-36

FOR THE FAMILY

Share the Scripture and promise with your family. Talk about what it takes for a runner to run a long race. Who sets up the race? What physical and emotional qualities are needed to run? What mental aspects get the runner to the finish line?

What does it mean to look to Jesus? How are you running today?

NOTES, REFLECTIONS, PRAYERS

Then the LORD said to him, "Who has made man's mouth? Who makes him mute, or deaf, or seeing, or blind? Is it not I, the LORD? Now therefore go, and I will be with your mouth and teach you what you shall speak."

EXODUS 4:11-12

HE WILL BE WITH YOU

On a Saturday we were getting ready for a college football game. I asked Terri, "What time are we taking Caitlin to your mom's?"

She responded, "Why wouldn't Caitlin go?"

I thought there was no reason to take her. The wheelchair would be hard to maneuver with thousands of people walking around. I would have to carry her up the stadium stairs. Would it matter to Caitlin if she went?

I am thankful how Terri made sure Caitlin was always with us. I would have left her with family. It would have been easier not to bring her. However, we carried her to the football game. Not only that, we took her to the beach, amusement parks, to the pool, on bike rides, family hikes, movies, everywhere we went. Thankfully, God used Terri to teach me to go where I needed to go. God sees our struggles, understands our dilemmas, and waits to see our response. When we go ahead, even though it might be difficult, our obedience glorifies Him.

Moses did not want to go either, much less face the struggles that he knew he would have to endure. However, God put him in the position and told him to go. But God did not send him alone. God was always there.

You may be facing new and different struggles; for example, a child with special needs, surgical scars, loss of hair, and other psychological and physical injuries.

However, God is with you as you go. No fear. No shame. Courage.

PRAY

Father, you are the Creator of heaven and earth. You have set our path before us. You even go ahead of us. Give us the courage we need to go forth. In the Name of Jesus, Amen.

Read further: Isaiah 42:16

FOR THE FAMILY

Share the reading and promise with your family. Talk about going on a Safari. What do you need? What will you see? How will you find your way? Discuss the importance of having a guide.

Your family is on a new adventure. That may be a challenge. God promises to be your guide. God promises to go with you.

How does God tell you to go? How does it make you feel that God goes with you?

NOTES, REFLECTIONS, PRAYERS

*This hope is a strong and trustworthy
anchor for our souls.*

HEBREWS 6:19 NLT

ANCHOR IN THE STORM

One day when Caitlin was seventeen years old, she had difficulty breathing. Her mom and sisters were in Uganda on a mission trip. Caitlin's face and lips were blue. I rushed her to the emergency room. Several nurses were stationed around the check-in area. The line was long. A nurse, writing, glanced up. She rushed to us, and said, "Follow me!" It was hard to keep up. She led us into a resuscitation room. Within seconds, the room was full of doctors and nurses. They started trying to stabilize Caitlin.

After thirty minutes, the attending doctor pulled me aside to give me an update on her condition. "Caitlin is dying," he said, "it is only a matter of minutes." The doctor had everyone clear a path for me. I knelt, placed my hand on Caitlin...and prayed.

The hospital chaplain asked, "Do you mind if I say a prayer of release?" Struggling with his words, I agreed.

Throughout this entire ordeal I felt an unexpected confidence upon me. "This is not going to be how Caitlin's story ends," I believed. I knew the love story between Caitlin, her mom and her sisters would not end without them being together.

Over the course of Caitlin's life, God had taught me to cast my hope on Him. Despite all I was being told, my trust was in Him. God was telling me He had a different plan. Minutes turned to hours. Finally, they sent us to a room. The last thing the doctor said was, "Caitlin will pass away this evening…"

The next day came. Caitlin's mom and sisters arrived back from Uganda. Caitlin became stable. Together, as a family, we returned home.

The anchor. When the storms of life come, what anchors you? Hebrews 6:19 says, "This hope is a strong and trustworthy anchor for our souls." Christ is the only anchor that holds. He fastens us to heaven. Hope. Hope in Christ keeps our hearts calm during the storm. Christ knows when the storm will stop before it even begins. Whatever the outcome, Christ is our anchor.

PRAY

Father, I cast all my hope on You and what You have done and what You will do for me and (_____) in Christ Jesus. I put my trust in Your promises. Anchor my soul in this storm with the hope found in Christ. Give me the peace that knows You are here. You are my confidence. Uphold me and strengthen me by this living hope. In the wonderful Name of Jesus, I pray, Amen.

Read Further: 1 Timothy 1:1; 1 Corinthians 12:21; 1 Peter 1:3

FOR THE FAMILY

Share the Scripture and reflect on the promise with your family. An anchor is designed to prevent a ship from drifting away due to wind and current. In order to be effective, the anchor must have the correct design, including the correct length for the depth of the water and it must be substantial enough to hold the ship.

There are many things in which we may place our hope: What are some of those things? What is Christ's promise to us when we weather the storms of life?

NOTES, REFLECTIONS, PRAYERS

_____

_____

_____

_____

_____

_____

_____

_____

HOPE

gathered

And the Holy Spirit helps us in our weakness. For example, we don't know what God wants us to pray for. But the Holy Spirit prays for us with groanings that cannot be expressed in words.

ROMANS 8:26 NLT

A PRAYER FOR YOU

Terri's comment surprised me. "I received a bizarre message on Caitlin's YouTube story today," she said.

"Really, what was it?" I asked.

"A lady in Trinidad asked, 'Do you really love Caitlin?'"

When we first had Caitlin, our prayer was: "Please God, let us go out and not have everybody stare, don't let Caitlin do anything to draw attention." Time and time again those prayers were not answered.

We cannot count the places she had projectile vomiting, or a complete blowout, or loud screaming seizures. All of which drew more attention than we wanted. The Spirit had amended our prayers. Over the years we began to see what the Spirit was, indeed, praying. "God, allow Caitlin to do what she needs to do to bring this family into conversations that allow people to see You."

Terri responded in such a way that God's Spirit moved in this lady's heart. She received Jesus as Lord and Savior. She was baptized, and joined a church. Terri later learned the entire story. The lady from Trinidad had planned to kill herself. When she saw Caitlin's video, she thought, "If this family can love a girl who cannot walk or talk, maybe someone can love me!" Terri introduced her to the One who does love all of us.

Having a special needs daughter, we did not know how to pray. In Romans 8:26, we are promised that the Spirit is at work revising our prayers and bringing them to God. Our prayer was that no one would notice our family. But the Spirit surprised us. He prayed for what we really needed and wanted. Because of His praying, we were taken out of our comfort zone. And through our experience, others saw their lives differently, too. All because of God's love.

PRAY

Father, I do not know exactly what to pray for (Romans 8:26). Sometimes I am overwhelmed. Thank You that the Spirit knows You and me and prays appropriately. I invited You to have Your way with my life. Your will be done. I admit I do not understand everything, but I trust You. In the Name of Jesus, I pray, Amen.

Read Further: One of the YouTube messages, from our friend in Trinidad (shown with her permission). English is not her primary language.

"That day when I saw the video of your daughter, I was thinking of my last meal. I felt trapped and hopeless, that I should not be here on earth anymore, but when I saw how you as parents cherished that life, immediately the choice of suicide became further away from my thoughts that day. I am glad that I stumbled across that video. Another thing too the way you responded to the email was even more amazing, you had me confused, when you stated, 'We have been blessed beyond what we could have ever chosen for ourselves!!!' And curiosity got the best of me, so I wanted to find out what made you so happy about that situation and hence, I email you again and found out you Serve Jesus Christ as your Lord and Savior and he made the difference in your life. And that's why I'm alive today: Jesus Christ is the difference."

YouTube Link:
https://www.youtube.com/watch?v=XyNEAhfnD6E

FOR THE FAMILY

Share the Scripture and reflect on the promise with your family. Talk about the doctors and their "rounds." In teaching hospitals, one person in the group is a medical student. The attending doctor lets the medical student present his diagnosis and recommendation. But there are times when the attending physician has to modify the student's analysis. Just like that medical student, we offer our prayer to God; however, our attending physician, the Holy Spirit, modifies our prayer for the most effective and proper treatment.

How does it make you feel realizing the Holy Spirit presents a refreshed prayer before God on your behalf?

NOTES, REFLECTIONS, PRAYERS

_____

_____

_____

_____

_____

_____

_____

_____

_____

_____

_____

_____

Now may our Lord Jesus Christ himself and God our Father, who loved us and by his grace gave us eternal comfort and a wonderful hope, comfort you and strengthen you in every good thing you do and say.

2 THESSALONIANS 2:16-17 NLT

HOPE DISPLACES DESPAIR

My daughter Macey worked her way towards me through the crowd. We embraced as she squeezed me with all her might. She was crying and trembling. It was going to be a difficult day.

We were attending the funeral service for our daughter Caitlin, Macey's sister. I was brokenhearted and wondering how to best comfort my family. When the graveside service concluded, people began to leave. Eventually, our family was all who remained. My emotions started racing. A parent should not have to attend their child's funeral. Grief filled me with anguish and I began to cry.

Three men came to bury my daughter. It was at that moment hope came. Jesus Christ would also one day come to take her body to heaven. Hope displaced my despair.

In 2 Thessalonians 2:16-17, we see the promise God has given us; namely, comfort that does not cease as well as hope that transcends death's despair. God has given us His Son. Through Christ, we see the Father's love for us and a hope that takes us farther in and higher up. Comfort and strength come when we are captivated by what God has done. As a result, hope rises, despair is displaced, and hearts are healed.

PRAY

Father God, when my heart is heavy, grant me a clearer vision of my hope in Christ that I may be comforted. Strengthen me with the confidence of knowing there will be a better day. I ask You to displace my desperation with the hope found in Christ. In Jesus' Name I pray, Amen.

Read Further: Habakkuk 1-3; Job 23:8-10; Hebrews 1:1-3

FOR THE FAMILY

Share the Scripture and promise with your family. We all know when someone comes into our hospital room at night because light pours into the room. Light displaces darkness. In the same way, God pours His comfort and hope into our hearts. The result is that hope rises and displaces despair.

How does hope affect our understanding, peace, and confidence in Christ?

NOTES, REFLECTIONS, PRAYERS

Hope Gathered

Along the Way

"I have said these things to you, that in me you may have peace. In the world you will have tribulation. But take heart; I have overcome the world."

JOHN 16:33

PEACE

My mother beat cancer, but not in the way most people would describe. Although cancer caused her a lot of pain and discomfort, it never took away the peace that she had in Christ Jesus. One of the medications took away her eyesight. Her first request for me, "Go get Bible audio cassettes so I can continue reading God's Word." God's promises were the eyes that showed her hope and peace. I will never forget telling her when the doctors said she only had a few days left. A glow came over her face. She smiled and said, "I get to see Jesus!" I was not a follower of Christ at that time, but after seeing the relationship she had, I wanted it, too.

In John 16:33, we see why the children of God can have peace no matter what this broken world brings. Jesus Christ is the Prince of peace. We can live in His peace by holding to what He has promised. Jesus says we live in a world of heartache and pain, but we may experience quiet confidence in our turmoil. As a child of God, we find the foundation of our assurance in what Christ has done. He has overcome the world. Through the cross of Christ, we have peace with God and are His children now and forever.

PRAY

*Lord Jesus, I place my hope at Your feet.
You have removed all that separates me
from You. What peace there is in Your
presence! Fill me with all the hope, joy,
and peace that is found only in You. You
have made me Your own. Now I know
the peace that passes all understanding.
In the beautiful Name of Jesus, I pray,
Amen.*

Read Further: John 14:27; 1 John 4:4; 5:4-5, 24;
Philippians 4:6-7; Romans 5:1

FOR THE FAMILY

Share the reading today and the promise with your family. Point to everything around you that needs electricity to work. Discuss what would happen if everything was unplugged from an electrical source. There is only one source of peace and comfort through difficult times—Jesus Christ. For us to have peace, we must be plugged into the Word and work of Jesus Christ.

How may we experience God's peace for now and eternity?

NOTES, REFLECTIONS, PRAYERS

And we know that for those who love God all things work together for good, for those who are called according to his purpose.

ROMANS 8:28

A PURPOSE IN EVERYTHING

My family and I watched an ice sculptor carve a dolphin in only a few minutes. It was pretty amazing. The sculptor started with just a block of ice. You could quickly see the resemblance of the dolphin as the sculptor chipped ice away. He was a master craftsman.

Romans 8:28 shows that God is a sculptor, too. God chiseled only one perfect image, His Son. He uses His children, whom He loves and who love Him, to shape them into the image of his Son. We often feel God's chiseling blows in our adversities, but the Apostle Paul says we can have confidence knowing God works each hardship on our behalf.

God collects all things together and uses them to work jointly on a common purpose. He unites the storms with the calm, the valleys and the peaks, to chisel away everything that does not look like His Son. As a Master craftsman, each strike is perfectly aimed to remove what does not fit. God forms us in the image of Christ. Sometimes it is painful. Sometimes it is a mystery, but His purpose is clear. You will become more like His Son.

PRAY

Father, I thank You that there is a purpose in everything. I trust that You are working for my good within this difficult season in my life. Comfort my heart with this promise that my hope will be found only in You. Help me to say, "Thy will be done." May I become more like Christ, in order to realize that all adversity will actually work out for my good. May others see His image in my brokenness to clearly show that hope is found only in Him. I pray in Jesus' Name, Amen.

Read Further: Philippians 3:7-21; 2 Corinthians 4:7-18

FOR THE FAMILY

Share the reading for today and the promise with your family. Flatten play-doh and place a man-shaped cookie cutter in the middle. Explain how the play-doh represents us and the cookie cutter, Christ. God wants us to look like His Son and has to peel away everything that does not look like Him. You can remove the excess play-doh as you explain. God uses both our good and bad days to make us look more like His Son. He is doing this so that others will see His Son through us. Etch your child's name on the play-doh image.

Why do we need things peeled away to look like Christ? What ways can you show Christ to others in the middle of this difficult time? Thank God for working everything for your good. Ask Him to use you to let others see Christ through your pain.

NOTES, REFLECTIONS, PRAYERS

_____

_____

_____

_____

_____

_____

_____

_____

_____

_____

_____

*"The LORD is my portion," says my soul,
"therefore I will hope in him."*

LAMENTATIONS 3:24

GOD IS ALL SUFFICIENT

One summer my daughter Megan came back from a mission trip to Africa. At the airport she said, "I have been urinating blood today, and someone said my eyes are yellow." I carried her to the hospital. Her eyes and face were orangish-yellow. Megan's liver was not functioning normally. A rash broke out over her body. For days Megan was tested for every infectious disease found in Africa. The doctors could not identify the underlying problem. Finally, the precise diagnosis and treatment came. Megan recovered.

During this desperate crisis, I experienced an extraordinary feeling of peace. That very week I had read Lamentations 3:24; God's Spirit imprinted its promise upon my heart. The result was a sense of peace that comforted us in our time of urgent need. God was everything we needed to calm our frayed nerves.

In Lamentations 3:24, the "weeping" Prophet Jeremiah knew suffering but also God's sufficiency. After having every earthly possession taken away, the Prophet's soul found hope in knowing he had the Lord. God was still sufficient for his most profound need and is enough for yours, too. God is ours. Our hearts may lift in the hope that we possess the One who controls every crisis.

PRAY

Father, where else am I to go? You are
all that I have and the only hope that can
give my heart peace. You are the hope
that does not fail. Give me rest in
knowing You are here and in control.
Though uncertainty surrounds me, may I
have the peace that comes from knowing
you are my God, and I belong to You. I
pray in Jesus' Name, Amen.

Read Further: Psalm 73:25; Romans 5:2, 5;
Proverbs 10:28

FOR THE FAMILY

Share the reading and promise with your family.
Discuss children that are wanting to play a game and
designating team captains. The captains are told to take
turns picking their teams. Their first pick is always going
to be the best player. Every team captain's hopes of
winning rise in proportion to the talent he or she gets on
their team. The promise is that God is on our team.
Whatever our crisis is, we have God and can trust in Him
to get us through.
Who is God? What does it mean to hope in God?
Why do we hope in God?

NOTES, REFLECTIONS, PRAYERS

I pray that God, the source of hope, will fill you completely with joy and peace because you trust in him. Then you will overflow with confident hope through the power of the Holy Spirit.

ROMANS 15:13 NLT

PROMISE OF HOPE

My daughter Courtney and two of her friends were in an accident. The young man who was with her took a severe blow to the head. The ambulance rushed him to the emergency room while his mother followed. The doctor finally came to the waiting room, "We need to scan for a brain bleed." The room went silent. Stunned.

"I can't wait to see what the Lord does with this," the mother said. Confident hope. Everyone was astonished.

I have never seen such incredible hope and trust in the Lord. The doctors were testing to see if this mother's son had a brain bleed. While scanning to see if he was dying, she was eager to see what God was doing. Her audacious hope was staring down an alarming adversity. Where did her hope come from?

The report came: no brain bleed. Her son eventually recovered completely.

In Romans 15:13, we see God as the possessor and provider of hope. By trusting Him we are filled with joy and peace. The promise follows: An overflowing sure hope that sees the unseen, fears no flame, and makes the world marvel.

PRAY

Father, I trust fully in You. I ask to be filled with the joy and peace that come from believing in Christ. You are my only real Hope. Overflow me by Your Holy Spirit so that my hope may triumph even when things don't go the way I expected. Draw close so I do not despair. Father, I need and trust in You. I cherish Your unfailing promises—they are the lifeline to my soul, and I am grateful. I pray in Jesus' Name, Amen.

Read Further: 2 Corinthians 3:12; Colossians 1:27; Hebrews 11:1; Daniel 3:8-30

FOR THE FAMILY

Share the Scripture and promise with your family. Discuss why some children in the hospital need oxygen.

In the same way, our spirit needs hope. In our most difficult times we feel desperate. Desperate for hope. The promise is that God, the source of all hope, will provide for us. Hope and trust embrace one another.

Why does hope come in the midst of desperate times? What does trusting God mean to you? If we don't get what we expected, what is the deeper meaning of hope?

NOTES, REFLECTIONS, PRAYERS

_____

_____

_____

_____

_____

_____

_____

_____

_____

_____

_____

*Trust in the LORD with all your heart,
and do not lean on your own
understanding. In all your ways
acknowledge him, and he will make
straight your paths.*

PROVERBS 3:5-6

PROMISE OF A BETTER PLAN

Injuries and sickness can shatter our plans. What are we to do when all we look forward to is abolished? Jason, a friend and Army Ranger, served in Afghanistan during Operation Enduring Freedom. He was an exceptional athlete who planned to serve in sports ministry but crippled his ankle while parachuting. The surgeon recommended amputation. Jason's plans were crippled as well.

While his life was ransacked, his reliance on God grew stronger. He could not lean on his foot, much less his own understanding of what to do. He was compelled to surrender to God. He sought God's plan for his life.

God led Jason not to get an amputation. Over time God worked a miracle in his foot and guided him where to place it. The foot the surgeon wanted to remove has been relocated overseas! Jason now travels mountain paths taking the gospel to remote and difficult places.

In Proverbs 3:5-6, we see that God promises to give a better path regardless of what cripples us. Sometimes he uses sickness and injury to lead. Our part is to trust Him without reservation. He leads. We follow. When our plans are torn, we turn to Him. He will guide us to a life filled with joy that is found in Christ.

PRAY

Father, I rely entirely on You. You are the source of all wisdom and worthy of my confidence and praise. I ask You to use this season of adversity to enable me to surrender my plans to You. Guide me so I will know the next step. May I recognize and travel the path You have for my life. In the Name of Jesus, I pray, Amen.

Read Further: Psalm 37:5; Proverbs 28:26

FOR THE FAMILY

Share the Scripture and promise with your family. Discuss how a coach prepares a game plan. He is the one who knows how the team needs to play. Any questions about the plan go to the coach.

In the same way, God offers a plan for our lives. Our decision is to trust Him with His purpose. When we do not know how to follow His plan, we ask for direction. As we believe and bring Him into every situation, the result is a life lived without vain regrets.

What will we experience when we trust the plan God offers for us?

NOTES, REFLECTIONS, PRAYERS

Have you not known? Have you not heard? The LORD is the everlasting God, the Creator of the ends of the earth. He does not faint or grow weary; his understanding is unsearchable.

ISAIAH 40:28

GOD KNOWS WHY

My daughter Megan moaned, "Daddy, I don't feel very well." I could tell from her facial expression she was in distress. I felt her forehead. She was on fire, with a temperature of 105°F. What was wrong? God, why have You allowed this to happen? We were serving You!

Megan and I were on a short-term mission trip to Africa, traveling with a ministry that saves orphan children who have no help or hope. These children are rescued and restored in Christ. We were doing the Lord's work.

We had never been in an African hospital. When we arrived, my concern grew greater. It was a shack. I wanted to take Megan home.

The nurse drew a blood sample for testing. A few minutes later the doctor delivered the diagnosis; Megan had malaria. She was given medicine, so our visit was brief. In a few days, she had recovered.

The doctors there treat malaria as often as ours treat a cold. I thought the better treatment would be found in America. God knew the proper care was in Africa. Thankfully, Megan's symptoms occurred in a place where the treatment was clear, and not where doctors might have wasted time trying to figure out the diagnosis. I was grateful that God understood what I did not.

"Why?" we often ask God. The promise in Isaiah 40:28, provides an answer. But sometimes God seems silent. When the prophet says, "His understanding is unsearchable," he is letting us know that some answers to "why?" are incomprehensible and would leave us confused. The prophet shows us the God who has always been and always will be, the God who brought all of creation into existence. This God who is all strength and the source of all we need, does, indeed, have the complete understanding of "why?"

Although we cannot understand, our pain somehow has a perfect place in His design. There is a "why?" that is for His glory and our good.

PRAY

Father, Your understanding is unsearchable. I do not grasp why this is going on, but I trust in You. Help me to rest in what You know. May knowing who You are bring comfort and hope when I feel faint. In Jesus' Name, I pray, Amen.

Read Further: Habakkuk 1-3; Job 23:8-10; Hebrews 1:1-3

FOR THE FAMILY

Share the Scripture and promise with your family. Talk about your trust in those who are in charge of our care; for example, drawing blood, giving medicine, and other procedures.

In what ways does God understand why this is happening? How does His knowledge and love make a difference in how we may look at this circumstance?

What do you think it means for God's understanding to be unsearchable?

NOTES, REFLECTIONS, PRAYERS

_____

_____

_____

_____

_____

_____

_____

_____

I wait for the LORD, my soul waits, and in his word I hope.

PSALM 130:5

THE LORD IS WORKING WHILE YOU WAIT

Medical tests and times of diagnoses demand our waiting. Times when impatience can invade our hope: Why can't they figure out what is going on? How much longer until we get the results back? Have they forgotten about us?

My daughter Courtney played tennis in high school. She practiced and played hard, on a pace to win a scholarship to college. But a shoulder injury interrupted her plans. The doctor ordered an MRI to determine what was damaged. Courtney asked, "Can I hit tomorrow?" The doctor responded, "Courtney, we have to figure out what is going on. You're going to have to wait." Wait she did. It took days to have the MRI, even more for the diagnosis. Her rotator cuff was torn, and so was her dream of achieving a scholarship for playing tennis. It would take months to heal.

The waiting was not wasted time, but an opportunity for weighing priorities. The Lord gave Courtney this waiting period, for reflection and to balance her life according to His Word rather than her world of tennis. After her recovery, tennis had better balance, and she did go on to play at a Christian college.

In Psalm 130:5 we are promised the Lord is at work even while we are waiting. Our part is to hope in that promise. Our season of waiting is not wasted; these are pauses when the Lord works to accomplish His promised purpose. We may cast our hope in His precious promises, for assurance in what He has said, confidence in what He has spoken.

PRAY

Father, I surrender to You while I wait. I know You are always working Your promises for me and in me through Christ Jesus. Capture my mind's attention so that my assurance will rest in You. Although I cannot comprehend what is going on, grant me confidence in You. May my hope rest in Your promises. In Jesus' Name, Amen.

Read Further: Romans 12:12; Micah 7:7; James 1:12; Psalm 40:1-3

FOR THE FAMILY

Share the Scripture and promise with your family. Waiting on medical tests can be frustrating because we don't see what is taking place to get the results.

In the same way, God promises to work during our waiting. In what way is waiting for God and waiting for results similar? God is never wasting time in your life. He uses the times we are still to enable us to see Him more clearly.

How may we grow closer to God as we wait?

NOTES, REFLECTIONS, PRAYERS

_____

_____

_____

_____

_____

_____

_____

_____

_____

_____

_____

_____

Love bears all things, believes all things,
hopes all things, endures all things.

1 CORINTHIANS 13:7

PROMISE THAT YOU CAN HELP

When sickness or disability shadows a child, a feeling of helplessness surrounds the parents. We watch as our child grows weak. Our children's pain and difficulties tear at us with panic and desperation. We want to help, but how? What can parents do as we depend on medical professionals?

In 1 Corinthians 13:7, we see the promise that you can provide a love for your child to lean on. During the bruising of our precious children, we apply the soothing care of love. The God of love, who has poured His love into our hearts, has given us a love that will sustain our children.

What does your child need? A parent who is strong in the present and sure of the promised future. This strength is shown when our love bears and endures. Love does not give up; love does not yield; love spreads a canopy of peace and strength over your child during the fiercest rain. No matter how severely the storm rages, a supporting love stands, like God's love.

Your child needs to witness a love reflecting reliability on the Lord. This kind of love will support them in fresh hope. Hope that rises from the great and precious promises that are found in Christ.

PRAY

Father, I thank You for the love You have poured into our hearts. I ask that Your love will enable us to provide what (_____) needs. Captivate our mind's attention and our heart's affections with Your deep, abiding love to nurture, soothe, and comfort (_____) heart and soul. Enable our love not to lose heart but to endure, not to lose faith but to hope. In the Name of Jesus, I pray, Amen.

Read Further: Romans 5:5; 2 Peter 1:4; Isaiah 42:3; 1 Corinthians 13; 2 Corinthians 1:3-7

FOR THE FAMILY

Share the Scripture and promise with your family. What did love look like in the life of Christ?

How can Christ's love for you bring comfort and encouragement to someone else?

NOTES, REFLECTIONS, PRAYERS

*[C]asting all your anxieties [worries] on
him, because he cares for you.*

1 PETER 5:7

HE CARES ABOUT OUR CONCERNS

Worry, anxiety and apprehension stir and unsettle us when our children are sick or disabled. The weight of worry makes us feel heavy and upset. Concern for our child's suffering and condition can crush our emotions.

Questions dominate our minds: "Why is there no improvement? What does this mean for my child's future? Do the doctors know what they are doing? How am I going to pay for this? How do I handle this crisis while caring for my other children? How can I deal with this and maintain my job?"

Feelings of doubt fill our hearts. We wonder, "God, why my child? Father, have You forgotten me? Do You not care about us?"

1 Peter 5:7 says, "casting all your anxieties (worries) on God, because He cares for you." We have a promise regarding all our concerns.

Here is God's promise: The burden we bear has His full attention. He carries all our worries as His priority. He wants to bear every care and concern alongside us.

Here is God's invitation: We may cast all we carry on Him. We may lay the weight of all our worries at His feet. He does not expect us to be self-reliant and to depend on our mere strength or resolve; instead, He invites us to experience the serenity of His loving, sovereign care. He will carry you and your concerns.

PRAY

Father, You know and see my every
concern. Grant me the comfort that
comes from knowing how much You
care. I lay all my anxiety and pain at
Your feet. I cannot carry this burden
alone. I surrender all to Your strength,
care, and complete understanding.
Thank you. In Jesus' Name I pray,
Amen.

Read Further: Hebrews 4:15; Psalm 119:116;
55:22; Proverbs 12:15

FOR THE FAMILY

Share the Scripture and promise with your family. Additionally, Luke 19:35 says the disciples threw their cloaks on a donkey for Jesus to ride upon. The word "throw" is the same word used here for us to "cast" our worries and cares upon God. The disciples cast their robes on the donkey and left them there. Like the disciples, God invites us to place our concerns upon Him and let Him carry them...and us.

What concerns do you want to cast upon God for Him to carry?

NOTES, REFLECTIONS, PRAYERS

For I know that as you pray for me and the Spirit of Jesus Christ helps me, this will lead to my deliverance.

PHILIPPIANS 1:19 NLT

PRAYER'S POWER

The most magnificent display of power I have ever seen was on a summer afternoon in Cape Canaveral. NASA was launching a SpaceX Falcon 9 rocket with over 6,000 pounds of supplies to the International Space Station. The Falcon 9 generates more than 1.7 million pounds of thrust. The rocket has been known to punch holes in the atmosphere for over 500 miles as it pushes its way into space.

My family and I had gathered miles away along with several others to watch. When the rocket took off everyone was excited and captivated by the intense flame thrusting into the sky. There was a couple near us that had seen several launches previously. They said, "Just wait." The crowd became silent. The sound of the engines had reached us. The noise vibrated our bodies. A crackling went through us. The launch was the greatest display of power we had ever seen.

When our child and family are faced with what seems impossible, we have access to a power far greater than the SpaceX Falcon 9. What power? Prayer!

Not long after Paul had started a church in Philippi, he wrote a letter to them from prison. In Philippians 1:19, we see the Apostle's assurance of his release tied to the prayers of these new believers. Paul was sent by Jesus to share the good news of God's power, the Gospel. Paul knew the power and necessity of prayer. He experienced answered prayers from ordinary people. Their prayers released God's power.

As God's children, our prayers carry the same power. God's power is displayed before, during, and after we pray. When we hold up our prayers and put our hope in God, He displays far more than we can imagine. Seeing a rocket's power hurtle it through space was an amazing experience. But to access God's power, we don't have to drive to a certain location or wait until it is time for the rocket to blast off. God's power constantly flows and is available 24/7 through prayer and belief in Jesus Christ.

PRAY

*Father, You have power over everything.
You care and want to be involved in
every detail of my life. I seek your
healing and helping hand to be on
(_____). I thank You for doing what
only You can. May my hope and trust be
strengthened through knowing that You
hear me. Whatever happens, I know the
power of Your presence is always
available through prayer. In Jesus'
Name, Amen.*

Read Further: 1 John 5:14-15; Psalm 17:6; Matthew 7:7-12; Ephesians 3:20; Daniel 13

FOR THE FAMILY

Share the Scripture and promise with your family. In times of medical emergency, we call 911. Talk about the resources standing by to respond to that call.

God also responds to our call to Him through prayers. How does He show His response? What should you be praying for?

NOTES, REFLECTIONS, PRAYERS

_____

_____

_____

_____

_____

_____

_____

_____

_____

HOPE
gathered

[H]e makes everything work out according to his plan.

THE LORD REIGNS

An expectant father asked me over lunch, "What advice would you have for us?" He was seeking to prepare his wife, his family, and himself for a new addition.

"Find the hope that comes from trusting in the sovereignty of God," I answered.

At his wife's 18-week checkup, the doctor saw something that concerned him. The waves of wearisome news began. The diagnosis was Trisomy 18. The family planned funeral arrangements for their son, David. Next, came the second but clear diagnosis, "Your son has Trisomy 21, Down Syndrome."

When David was born, he could not breathe on his own. Fluid surrounded and suffocated his lungs. His condition was critical and he remained in NICU[3] for eleven weeks. He could not breathe without a ventilator, and he could not eat; he would clamp down on his breathing tube and lose consciousness. His heart would stop. Yet, in the midst of these complications, he began to improve. David was able to go home but needed heart surgery within three months.

David's heart was repaired, but the medical complications returned. The doctors said David needed transferring to another hospital specializing in his unique

---

[3] Neonatal Intensive Care Unit

condition. Beyond explanation or understanding, he again started to improve. David, again, went home with his family.

As my wife and I visited them in the hospital room, David's dad mentioned the lunch we'd had. "Tommy, I cannot tell you how many times I keep going back to the sovereignty of God; He is all we need, and He has been my anchor of faith."

In Ephesians 1:11, we have the promise that God is sovereign: He reigns over and guides all things. God's divine desire, although sometimes mysterious, is being worked out lovingly, wisely, in every circumstance. When we journey through the storms of life, we may trust the One who knows us and guides us. As we do, hope will fill our hearts and anchor our faith.

PRAY

Father, I acknowledge that You reign over all that comes my way. May I trust Your love for me. You allow the storms of life, but You also are with me in the storm. Grant the comfort and peace that comes from knowing You are in me—and You are in full control. In Jesus' Name I pray, Amen.

Read Further: Psalm 135:6; Hebrews 1:3; Proverbs 16:33; Philippians 4:4-7

FOR THE FAMILY

Share the Scripture and promise with your family. Talk about a time when you were surprised by an inclement weather event and had to seek whatever shelter you could find. Maybe the shelter wasn't what you wanted but it was enough. It was plenty. The promise is that God is the One who provided that shelter for you. It was there all along.

How does knowing God is in control of all things bring you comfort?

NOTES, REFLECTIONS, PRAYERS

_____

_____

_____

_____

_____

_____

_____

_____

ACKNOWLEDGEMENTS

I want to thank...

My Lord and Savior Jesus Christ who is my portion in whom my soul hopes;

Coach Gene Stallings for graciously coming alongside this book project and being a great role model for all us fathers with children who have special needs;

Dr. Langston Haygood for encouraging me to put to paper that which was put on my heart and for being with me every step of the way;

The Shufflebargers for being part of our family in every way;

Allen and Sarah Nunnally for loving us, their willingness to help, and for all the value they brought to this book project. We love you guys and are blessed to call you family;

Jason Haley for being a constant encouragement that nothing can stop what the Spirit leads us to do;

Suzanne Owens for being such a special part of our Caitlin story;

Lesa Gibson for showing us all what unshakeable faith looks like;

The Moss family for their encouragement and reminder of what it looks like having a child with special needs who is critically ill while holding onto the promises that are in Christ;

All those who loved and cared for Caitlin while being there when we needed them. We could not have done it without you.

ABOUT THE AUTHOR

Tommy and his wife, Terri, have four children and live in the Birmingham, Alabama area. He is involved in several Christian ministries with both a local and global focus. He serves as the Chairman of the Board for Sozo Children (*http://www.sozochildren.org/*) and he enjoys traveling to teach at remote Bible Institutes in various countries for World Reach (*http://world-reach.org/*).

Tommy works as a partner in an engineering and mechanical construction company. He has a degree in Mechanical Engineering, is also a licensed Professional Engineer, and completed his master's degree in Christian Ministry.

If you would like to contact Tommy about *Hope Gathered* or want to see Caitlin's story, visit his website at www.hopegathered.com. You can also reach him by email at tommy@hopegathered.com.

Made in the USA
Columbia, SC
10 April 2019